MACMILLAN READER

PRE-INTERMEDIATE LEVEL

WILLIAM SHAKESPEARE

A Midsummer Night's Dream

Retold by Rachel Bladon

macmillan education

Macmillan Readers is a series of engaging narrative texts designed to stimulate learners while enhancing their language skills, building literacy and boosting reading confidence. Through captivating stories and fascinating cultural themes, learners will explore a diversity of scenarios that foster vocabulary expansion, comprehension skills and a lifelong love of reading.

The right reader at every stage

Tailored to each learner's stage of language proficiency, our six levels feature text adapted to match the skill level. With controlled vocabulary and grammar, learners can read freely and immerse themselves in the story. When more challenging words are introduced, either the text will provide sufficient context to aid understanding or a full explanation will be provided in the Glossary.

Readers for all, anywhere, anytime

Macmillan Readers are perfect for shared, guided and independent reading. Whether in traditional print, immersive audio or the convenient eBook, Macmillan Readers are equally effective for in-class activities, paired discussions or solo reading at home or on the move.

Reading for pleasure, knowledge and well-being

Regular reading and reading for pleasure:

- increases reading confidence, benefiting all literacy skills, not just reading.
- reinforces and enriches vocabulary, providing a variety of contexts.
- expands general knowledge.
- supports concentration, inner reflection and well-being.

Macmillan Readers will inspire a love for reading in English while nurturing essential language skills. Unlock new worlds, expand horizons and embark on an adventure in English!

(NOTE: While the content of Macmillan Readers is evaluated for age suitability, we kindly remind parents and teachers that they are ultimately responsible for determining whether a particular book is appropriate for their child or student.)

Contents

A Note About the Author

William Shakespeare is believed to be the greatest English writer of all time. He was born in Stratford upon Avon, in England, in April 1564. His father was a wealthy merchant – he bought and sold wool and leather. In December 1582, Shakespeare married Anne Hathaway, the daughter of a farmer, and they had three children. We know very little about Shakespeare's early life. Some people believe that he worked as a teacher. Other people think that he became a member of a travelling group of actors. But we do know that by 1592, Shakespeare was living in London. By then, he had already become quite well known as an actor and a playwright[1].

At that time, in the early 1590s, the first theatres were just opening in England. In 1593, these new theatres and their actors had a difficult year. The theatres were often closed because of the plague – a disease which killed many people. But the following year, Shakespeare joined a new group of actors called The Lord Chamberlain's Men, and they became very successful.

In 1598, the Lord Chamberlain's Men built their own theatre, The Globe, which was unusual because it had a round shape.

Theatres at that time were very different to the modern theatres of today. There was no scenery and no curtain, and there were no intervals[2] or breaks between scenes. Women were not allowed to act, so their roles were played by boys. Most of the theatres did not have roofs, so plays were only shown in good weather and in daylight.

In 1603, Queen Elizabeth died, and James I became the King of England. King James liked Shakespeare's work very much, so he asked Shakespeare's group of actors to work for him. After that, they were called the King's Men, and they often performed[3] plays for the King. In about 1607, Shakespeare stopped acting. After that time he lived mostly in Stratford. He had become very wealthy, and was a very important person in Stratford. He died there on his birthday, in 1616.

Shakespeare wrote about 37 plays, including *A Midsummer Night's Dream*, *Romeo and Juliet*, *Hamlet* and *Macbeth*. He also wrote many beautiful poems.

Many of Shakespeare's plays were only published as books after his death. In Shakespeare's time, people used to write plays very quickly. The actors performed them a few times and then they threw them away. No one really thought of keeping plays for people to read. Because of this, the plays of Shakespeare that we read today are probably not exactly the same as the ones that he first wrote.

Shakespeare used many different styles of writing in his plays. He was very clever at writing beautiful poetry, and he could use words to make pictures of things in people's minds. His plays showed very clearly what was going on in the world, and the people in them always seemed very real. Because of this, Shakespeare's plays are still performed all over the world today, and people in schools, colleges and universities have been studying his work for many years.

A Note About This Play

William Shakespeare wrote *A Midsummer Night's Dream* more than four hundred years ago, in about 1595 (we do not know the exact year). It is a play about love and marriage. Somebody probably asked Shakespeare to write the play for an important wedding. *A Midsummer Night's Dream* was probably performed for the first time at that wedding.

The play is about things that happened in Greece in ancient[4] times, thousands of years ago. It is not a true story. However, two of the main characters[5] in the play, Theseus and Hippolyta, are from very ancient Greek stories. The play begins and ends in Athens, the main city of Greece. The rest of the play takes place in a wood outside the city.

In *A Midsummer Night's Dream* there are two different worlds: the real world and the world of the fairies. Oberon and Titania are the King and Queen of the fairies, and there are other fairy characters in the play, including Puck. The fairies have strange powers, and people from the real world cannot see them. Puck loves to cause trouble for people, so he often uses his special fairy powers to play tricks on them.

There are four main groups of characters in the play, but the story brings them all together. As well as the fairies, there is a group of young lovers (Helena, Demetrius, Hermia and Lysander). We also meet Theseus (the Duke of Athens) and Hippolyta, who are getting ready for their wedding, at the beginning and end of the play.

Finally there is a group of craftsmen[6] who are practising a play. They hope that their play will be performed at Theseus and Hippolyta's wedding. The craftsmen are the funniest characters in *A Midsummer Night's Dream*. They have written a very bad play, and they are not very good at acting!

Shakespeare always has important themes, or subjects, in his plays. The main theme of this play is love and marriage. Each group of characters in the play shows something different about the theme. The four lovers show what love is like when you are very young. Theseus and Hippolyta are older, and are getting ready for their wedding. Oberon and Titania have had an argument and their marriage is going through a difficult time. Even the craftsmen are practising a play about love!

A Midsummer Night's Dream is also about the difference between the real world and the imaginary world – the world of fairies. Many of the things that happen in the play are like things that happen in dreams. And the characters are not sure whether these things have really happened or not!

This Version of
A Midsummer Night's Dream

This version of *A Midsummer Night's Dream* includes some 'real' extracts of text. We hope that they will help the students to both understand, and enjoy, Shakespeare in the original. The extracts follow immediately after their simplified form. They are shaded in grey and have a separate glossary. In the glossary, words that are old English (no longer used) appear in *italics*. See the example (from page 19) below:

Fairy: Over hills, over valleys,[22] and across the countryside. I go everywhere, faster than the moonlight. I work for Titania, the Queen of the Fairies. My job is to find some dewdrops[23]. I will put them on the grass because Queen Titania and the other fairies are coming here later.

simplified text

Fairy: *Over hill, over dale,*
Thorough bush, thorough brier,
Over park, over pale,
Thorough flood, thorough fire,
I do wander every where,
Swifter than the Moon's sphere;

original text

dale = valley
thorough = through
brier = rosebush
pale = land with a fence around it
flood = when the land is covered with too much water
wander = travel around with nothing special to do
swifter = faster
sphere = round object

glossary

The People in This Story

There are a few characters from Shakespeare's *A Midsummer Night's Dream* who do not appear in this Macmillan Reader. In Shakespeare's play, there are two extra craftsmen called **Snout** and **Starveling** who practise 'Pyramus and Thisbe' with Quince, Flute, Snug and Bottom. We have tried to keep this Reader as simple as possible, and so we have not included Snout and Starveling. Some of the things that Snout and Starveling say in Shakespeare's play are said by the other craftsmen. Theseus's attendant **Philostrate** and Titania's fairies **Peaseblossom, Cobweb, Moth** and **Mustardseed** also do not appear in this Reader.

The Athenian Court

The Lovers (continued)
Lysander falls in love with
loves
Demetrius
Helena
The Fairy Kingdom
Oberon
Puck
applies magic to
Titania
The Craftsmen
Quince
Flute
Bottom
Snug

Act 1, Scene 1

[Near the Duke's palace[7] in Athens. Enter the Duke Theseus, with Hippolyta]

Theseus: It is only four days until our wedding, fair[8] Hippolyta. But each day goes so slowly.

Hippolyta: Those four days will quickly turn into nights. And we will quickly dream away those nights. And then it will be time for our wedding.

Theseus: I want Athens to be full of happiness on our wedding day. We shall have dancing, singing and great celebrations!

[Enter Egeus and his daughter Hermia with Lysander and Demetrius]

Egeus: *[to Theseus]* Good day, my lord[9]. I hope you are well.

Theseus: I am very well, thank you, Egeus. What is your news?

Egeus: My lord, I am very angry with my daughter, Hermia. Demetrius, step forward!

[Demetrius comes forward]

This is Demetrius. I have told Demetrius that he can marry my daughter. But now she has fallen in love with another man. Lysander, come here!

[Lysander comes forward]

Lysander, you have made Hermia fall in love with you. You have sung love songs outside her window at night. You have given her presents. You have pretended[10] that you are in love with her. You have stolen her heart and now she will not obey me. Theseus, my lord, I want to give Hermia a warning. This is my warning: she must marry Demetrius, or she must die. That is the law of Athens.

Theseus: Hermia, you should always obey your father. Your father wants you to marry Demetrius. And Demetrius is a good man. Why won't you marry him?

Hermia: I want to choose my own husband. I love Lysander, and I want to marry him. I wish my father would see things through my eyes.

Theseus: No, you must look through your father's eyes when you choose your husband. And your father has chosen Demetrius. You must marry him.

Hermia: I am sorry, my lord. You are our duke, and I should not talk like this to you. But please can you tell me one thing? What will happen to me if I will not marry Demetrius?

Theseus: You must die, or become a nun[11]. And if you become a nun, you can never be with a man again. So, think carefully, Hermia. Do you want to spend your life shut away inside, praying[12] to the cold moon?

Hermia: I will live, grow old and die as a nun if I have to. But I will not marry Demetrius. I do not love him.

Theseus: Please think about this for a few days, Hermia. In four days, it is your wedding. On that day, you must promise to marry Demetrius. This is what your father wants. If you won't obey your father, you must become a nun, or die.

Demetrius: Do what your father says, sweet Hermia. *[to Lysander]* Hermia is mine. Don't try to take her from me.

Lysander: Hermia's father loves you, Demetrius! Why don't you marry him? And let me marry Hermia: *[to Egeus]* My lord, I would be a good husband to Hermia. I come from a good family, like Demetrius. And I have plenty of money. In every way, I am as good as him. But most importantly, I love Hermia. And I will say this in front of Demetrius. Demetrius was in love with Helena before he met Hermia. And poor Helena is still in love with him! You cannot trust Demetrius. He is always changing his mind.

Theseus: Yes, I also heard this about Demetrius and Helena. I wanted to talk about it with Demetrius, but I have been too busy. Demetrius and Egeus, come with me. I want to talk to you both alone. Fair Hermia, your father has chosen a husband for you. You must try to love him, or you must die, or become a nun. That is the law of Athens. *[Hippolyta looks upset]* Don't worry, Hippolyta, my love. Demetrius! Egeus! Let's go and talk about this together. Also, I need you to help me get some things ready for our wedding.

Egeus: We will follow you, my lord.

[Exit Theseus, Hippolyta, Demetrius and Egeus]

Lysander: Hermia, my love, you look so pale. Your cheeks were once like roses. But now those roses are dying.

Hermia: I want to cry, and my tears would be like rain.

Lysander: In every story about true love[13] that I have ever heard, there have always been problems. Sometimes the two lovers come from very different families. Sometimes one of the lovers is much older than the other. And sometimes the lovers' friends do not like their choice. But even when there are none of these problems, other things can happen. War, death or illness can destroy love. And then love is as short as a dream, and as quick as lightning.

Lysander: *The course of true love never did run smooth.*

course = the way that things happen

Hermia: If all true lovers have problems like these, then we can face our problems too. Love brings dreams, and thoughts, but tears as well.

Lysander: That is a good way to think. Listen, Hermia. I have a very rich aunt who lives far from Athens. She doesn't have any children, and I am like a son to her. Let's run away and stay with her. The law of Athens is not important there, so we can get married. If you love me, run away from your father's house tomorrow night. I will wait for you in the palace wood outside Athens. Do you remember that wood? I met you there with Helena one May morning.

Hermia: Lysander, I promise that I will meet you there.

Lysander: Don't break your promise. *[Sees Helena]* Look, here comes Helena.

[Enter Helena, in a hurry]

Hermia: Where are you going, fair Helena?

Helena: Fair? Don't call me fair. Demetrius only loves your beauty. He doesn't love me. To Demetrius, your eyes are like stars, and your voice is more beautiful than the song of the sweetest bird. I wish I could talk like you. I wish I could look like you. I wish I could be you! Then perhaps Demetrius would love me. Please teach me to be like you! How did you make Demetrius love you? Please show me!

Hermia: I am not friendly or kind to him. But the more I hate him, the more he loves me.

Helena: I wish I could make him love me. But the more I love him, the more he hates me!

Hermia: I never wanted him to love me, Helena.

Helena: I know. I don't blame[14] you. I blame your beauty. And I wish I was as beautiful as you.

Hermia: *I frown upon him, yet he loves me still.*
Helena: *O that your frowns would teach my smiles such skill.*
Hermia: *I give him curses, yet he gives me love.*
Helena: *O that my prayers could such affection move.*
Hermia: *The more I hate, the more he follows me.*
Helena: *The more I love, the more he hateth me.*
Hermia: *His folly Helena is no fault of mine.*
Helena: *None but your beauty, would that fault were mine.*

frown = lower your eyebrows to show that you are angry or annoyed
skill = being able to do something well
curses = words that wish bad things for someone
affection = love
hateth = hates
folly = silly behaviour
would = I wish

Hermia: Don't worry, Helena. After tomorrow, Demetrius will never see my face again. Lysander and I are going to run away. Before I met Lysander, I loved Athens. But now he has made it a terrible place for me. Do you remember that we often used to go to that wood outside Athens, Helena? We used to lie among the flowers, telling each other secrets. Lysander and I are going to meet in that wood tomorrow night. We are going to start a new life away from Athens. Goodbye, my dear friend. Please think of us. And I hope that Demetrius will fall in love with you once more. Meet me tomorrow, Lysander. Oh, I can't wait to be with you again!

[Exit Hermia]

Lysander: I will see you then, my Hermia. Goodbye, Helena. I hope that Demetrius will love you as much as you love him.

[Exit Lysander]

Helena: *[to herself]* Hermia and Lysander are so happy together. I wish I could be as happy as them. But Demetrius doesn't love me anymore. He loves Hermia. Everyone in Athens thinks that I am as beautiful as Hermia. But Demetrius doesn't agree. He doesn't listen to what other people say. And I love Demetrius in the same way – I cannot see the truth. I cannot see any bad things in him: to me he is perfect. Love is blind – it cannot see. And it is like a child. When people are in love, they often don't know what they are doing. Before Demetrius saw Hermia, he told me that he was mine. But then he fell in love with her and forgot all about me. *[Making a decision]* I am going to tell Demetrius that Hermia is leaving Athens tomorrow night. He will follow her to the wood. I shouldn't tell him Hermia's secret. But I can't stop myself. Although it will hurt me again, it means that I will see him once more.

Act 1, Scene 2

[Enter the craftsmen – Quince, Snug, Bottom, and Flute]

Quince: Is everybody here? We have met here today to rehearse[15] a play for the Duke's wedding day. Now, here is a list of the parts[16] that everyone will play.

Bottom: Peter Quince, why don't you tell us what the play is about first? Then you can read out the parts.

Quince: Our play is a terribly sad comedy[17] about the death of Pyramus and Thisbe.

Bottom: It's a wonderful play – and very funny! Now Peter Quince, call out everyone's name.

Quince: *[Calling the names]* Nick Bottom!

Bottom: I'm ready! What is my part?

Quince: You, Nick Bottom, will be Pyramus.

Bottom: Who is Pyramus? Is he a lover or a cruel[18] leader?

Quince: He is a lover who bravely kills himself for love.

Bottom: *[A little disappointed]* I would prefer to be a cruel leader. But if I have to be a lover, I shall play the part perfectly. There will be real tears, and plenty of sadness. What are the other parts?

Quince: Francis Flute?

Flute: Yes, Peter Quince.

Quince: Flute, you will play Thisbe.

Flute: Who is Thisbe? A brave horseman?

Quince: No, Thisbe is the lady that Pyramus loves.

Flute: *[Shocked]* A lady? I can't play a lady! I have a beard.

Quince: That doesn't matter. You can cover your face with a mask[19]. You can speak very quietly. Then you will sound like a lady.

Bottom: I could play Thisbe too. I'll speak very quietly, like this: *[Whispers]* 'Ah Pyramus, my lover, dear.'

Quince: No, Bottom. You must play Pyramus. And Flute, you must play Thisbe. Snug, are you here?

Snug: Yes, Peter Quince.

Quince: Snug, you will play the lion.

Snug: Have you already written the lion's part, Peter Quince? I am a very slow learner. I will need to practise a lot.

Quince: You won't need to practise, Snug. The lion does not say anything. It only roars[20].

Bottom: Let me play the lion too, Quince. I shall roar loudly. I shall roar so well that the Duke will say, 'Roar again, lion! Roar again!'

Quince: No, Bottom. You would roar too loudly. The ladies would all be frightened, and they would scream. And then the Duke would send us away.

Bottom: Then I shall roar gently like a little bird.

Quince: No, Bottom. You will play Pyramus. You cannot play any other part. Pyramus is a fine man, a very polite man, and so you must play Pyramus.

Bottom: *[Proudly[21]]* You say that Pyramus is a fine man? Well, all right then, I shall play Pyramus. How should I wear my beard? I could have a long beard, a short beard, a black beard or a brown beard.

Quince: *[Laughing]* Or you could have no beard at all. Now, here are your parts, everybody. Please learn them before tomorrow. Meet me in the palace wood outside town tomorrow night after dark. No one will see us there, and we can rehearse secretly.

All: We shall be there!

Act 2, Scene 1

[The palace wood, near Athens. Puck is sitting by a tree. Enter a fairy]

Puck: Hello, Fairy. Where are you going?

Fairy: Over hills, over valleys[22], and across the countryside. I go everywhere, faster than the moonlight. I work for Titania, the Queen of the Fairies. My job is to find some dewdrops[23] I will put them on the grass because Queen Titania and the other fairies are coming here later.

> **Fairy:** *Over hill, over dale,*
> *Thorough bush, thorough brier,*
> *Over park, over pale,*
> *Thorough flood, thorough fire,*
> *I do wander everywhere,*
> *Swifter than the Moon's sphere;*
>
> dale = valley
> *thorough* = through
> brier = rosebush
> pale = land with a fence around it
> flood = when the land is covered with too much water
> wander = travel around with nothing special to do
> swifter = faster
> sphere = round object

Puck: Oberon, the King of the Fairies, is spending the evening here tonight. Make sure that Titania doesn't come near him because he is very cross with her. Titania has a little Indian boy, and Oberon wants him. He wants to take the boy with him when he travels. But Titania loves the little boy, and keeps him with her all the time. She won't let Oberon take him. Every time Titania and Oberon meet, they argue about the little boy. They become so angry that they frighten the fairies. Then the fairies hide in acorn cups[24].

Fairy: Wait a minute. Aren't you Puck? I have heard all about you. You cause mischief[25] everywhere. You frighten young girls; you steal the cream from the milk; in the night you make people get lost.

Puck: *[Laughing]* You are right. I am that happy traveller of the night. I am Oberon's fairy, and my jokes make him laugh. Sometimes, when I see someone who talks too much, I hide in their drink. Then when they pick up their glass, I jump up and pour the drink all over them! Or when I see a wise old woman telling stories, I sometimes pretend to be a chair. When she tries to sit down on the chair, I jump away, and she falls on the floor. Then everyone laughs and says it is the funniest thing they have ever seen! *[Stops and listens]* But stand back, Fairy. Here comes Oberon.

Fairy: *[Looking through the wood]* Oh no. Here comes Titania.

[Enter Oberon and Titania from different sides, with their fairies]

Oberon: I am sorry to meet you here in the moonlight, proud Titania.

Titania: *[Seeing Oberon]* Is it you, jealous Oberon? Come on, fairies, let's go.

Oberon: Wait! I am your husband, aren't I?

Titania: Then I suppose I must be your wife. What are you doing here? Let me guess! Hippolyta, who you are in love with, is getting married to Theseus soon. I expect that you have come here to bless[26] her wedding bed!

Oberon: How can you talk about my friendship with Hippolyta like that? I know all about you and Theseus. You have always tried to stop him being with other women. Everyone can see that you are in love with him!

Titania: You are telling lies, because you are jealous! Ever since the beginning of summer, everywhere I go, you come and argue with me. Every time my fairies and I try to dance to the music of the wind, you stop us. And so now the winds have become angry with us. They do not want to play their music if no one will dance. They have stirred up thick fogs, which have turned into rain and filled the rivers. The rivers have covered the land, the crops[27] have gone bad and the animals have died. The moon, angry at our arguments, has washed the air, and now the seasons are all confused[28]. Is it spring, summer, autumn, or winter? The red roses are covered in ice. And sweet summer buds[29] grow in the middle of winter. And this is all our fault[30]. This is all because of our arguments.

Oberon: You can change it if you stop arguing with me. I am not asking you for very much. I just want that little child to be my servant[31] boy.

Titania: Stop thinking about that little boy. I will not let anyone take him from me. And I'll tell you why. His mother was a great friend of mine. We used to sit on the beach together in India at night. We told each other secrets as we watched the ships go out to sea. But she died when her baby boy was born. And so now I am looking after that little boy for her. And because of her, I will not let anyone take him from me.

Oberon: How long are you staying here in the palace wood?

Titania: I shall probably stay here until after Theseus's wedding. If you stop arguing, then you can stay with us.

Oberon: Give me that boy, and I will stay with you.

Titania: Never! Not even if you gave me the whole of Fairy Land. Let's go, fairies. If we stay here any longer, I shall get very angry.

[Exit Titania and her fairies]

Oberon: Go, then! But you will be sorry that you have not obeyed me! *[Suddenly has an idea]* Puck, come here. I once showed you a special purple flower. Do you remember? If you put the juice of the flower in someone's eyes while they are sleeping, something strange happens. When the person wakes up, they fall in love with the next thing they see! Go and get me some of this juice, as quickly as you can.

Puck: I will bring you some in less than an hour. *[Puck leaves]*

Oberon: *[to himself]* When I have the juice, I shall find Titania and wait until she is asleep. Then I shall put some juice in her eyes. *[Laughing]* And she will fall in love with the next thing she sees when she wakes up! Perhaps she will fall in love with a lion, or a bear – or a monkey! I know another special flower which can break the love spell[32]. It stops people being in love like this. But I won't give this flower to Titania until she promises to give me her little boy. *[Listens]* There are some people coming! I am a fairy, so people cannot see me. I'll stay here and listen to their conversation.

Oberon: *Having once this juice,*
I'll watch Titania, when she is asleep,
And drop the liquor of it in her eyes:
The next thing then she waking looks upon,
(Be it on lion, bear, or wolf, or bull,
On meddling monkey, or on busy ape)
She shall pursue it, with the soul of love.

liquor = liquid
bull = a male cow
meddling = playing around with other people's things
ape = a large monkey without a tail
pursue = follow
soul = strong feeling

[Enter Demetrius, followed by Helena]

Demetrius: *[to Helena]* I do not love you, so stop following me! Where is Lysander, and where is fair Hermia? You told me that they had run away to this wood. So I have come here to find them. But I cannot find Hermia, and now I am mad with anger. Go away! Leave me alone, and stop following me!

Helena: Your heart is like iron[33]. It is a cold, hard, magnet[34] and it pulls my heart towards it. Stop pulling me with your heart, and I will stop following you.

Demetrius: Do I say nice things to you? Do I call you beautiful? I have told you already that I do not love you.

Helena: And because you do not love me, I love you more. I am like a little dog who loves his master[35]. The more you are cruel to me, the more I love you. So treat me like your dog! Turn away from me, hit me, treat me badly! But let me follow you. Is that too much to ask? It is enough for me.

Demetrius: I feel sick when I see you.

Helena: And I feel sick when I don't see you.

Demetrius: You should not have come here, with someone who does not love you. It is not right for a young woman to come to a lonely place at night.

Helena: When I see your face, night turns into day. So it is not night now! And you are like the whole world to me. So this wood isn't lonely, because the whole world is here.

Demetrius: I have had enough of this. Let me go. And if you follow me, you will not feel safe in this wood! I may harm you!

Helena: You harm me wherever I go. Love is not fair for women. We cannot fight for love like men. We have to be chased[36], we cannot chase.

[Exit Demetrius]

I'll follow you. Even if you killed me, it would still make me happy, because I love you so much.

[Exit Helena]

Oberon: Don't worry, young Helena. Before that young man leaves this wood, I shall turn everything around. I shall make sure that you are running away from him, and that he is looking for your love.

[Enter Puck]

Oberon: Hello there, Puck. Did you find the flower?

Puck: Yes, here it is.

Oberon: Give it to me, Puck. *[Puck gives Oberon a flower]* There is a beautiful hillside near here, covered in flowers. Titania often likes to sleep there after an evening of dancing. I shall go and find her there, and put some love juice in her eyes while she is sleeping. *[Laughing]* And then, I hope, she will fall in love with something horrible! You take some too, Puck. *[Breaking off a bit of the flower and giving it to Puck]* There are two young people in the wood. A gentle lady from Athens is in love with a man who does not want to be with her. Find him, and put some love juice in his eyes. And make sure that the lady is the first person he will see when he wakes up. You cannot miss him, because he is wearing Athenian[37] clothes. Do this, and then meet me here at dawn – when the sun comes up.

Oberon: *A sweet Athenian lady is in love*
With a disdainful youth: anoint his eyes,
But do it when the next thing he espies,
May be the Lady. Thou shalt know the man,
By the Athenian garments he hath on.

disdainful = treating other people as if they are not important
youth = young person
anoint = put liquid on the body
espies = sees
Thou = you
shalt = shall
garments = clothes
hath = has

Puck: I shall do what you ask, my lord.

[Exit Oberon and Puck]

Act 2, Scene 2

[Enter Titania with her fairies]

Titania: Come on, fairies. Let's sing and have a dance. And then you must go and do your work. You must kill the bugs[38] on the rosebuds. You must find bats'[39] wings to make fairy coats. And you must keep away the night owls[40]. Sing me to sleep now. Then go and do your work, and let me rest.

[Fairies sing; Titania sleeps]

Fairy: The Queen is asleep. One fairy will watch over her. The rest of us must go! *[One fairy stands next to Titania, and the others leave]*

[Enter Oberon. His fairies quietly take away the fairy who is watching over Titania]

Oberon: *[Puts love juice in Titania's eyes]* When you wake, you will fall in love with the first thing you see. A cat, or a bear, or a hairy pig will be your love! *[Laughing]* I hope you wake up when something horrible is walking past!

[Exit Oberon; Enter Lysander and Hermia]

Lysander: My love, we have walked in the woods for a long time. You are tired, and I am afraid that we are lost. Let's rest here for the night. We'll set off again in the morning.

Hermia: Yes, Lysander. I shall lie down right here. *[Lies down on the grass]* Sleep well, my love.

Lysander: *[Lies down next to Hermia]* I shall lie here next to you. Our hearts are like one, so we need only one bed.

Hermia: No, good Lysander. Please don't sleep so close to me. Lie over there. *[Points to a place a little way away]*

Lysander: I only have good reasons for wanting to lie next to you. Our hearts are so close that they feel like one heart.

Hermia: I know, Lysander. But we are not married yet. And so it is not right for us to lie next to each other. Lie down over there, and good night, sweet friend. I hope that you will love me until you die!

Lysander: I could not live if I stopped loving you. *[Moves a little way off and lies down]* I shall lie down here. Sleep well.

[They sleep. Enter Puck]

Puck: I have searched the whole forest, but I have not found an Athenian man to use this love juice on. *[Sees Lysander lying on the grass]* Wait a moment, who is this? This man is wearing Athenian clothes. He must be the man who Oberon was talking about! He must be the man who was so unkind to the young Athenian lady. *[Sees Hermia]* And here is the young lady herself, asleep on the dirty wet ground! Poor woman, she doesn't dare to lie next to that cruel man. *[Puts love juice in Lysander's eyes]* Love juice, do your job! *[Laughing, to Lysander]*

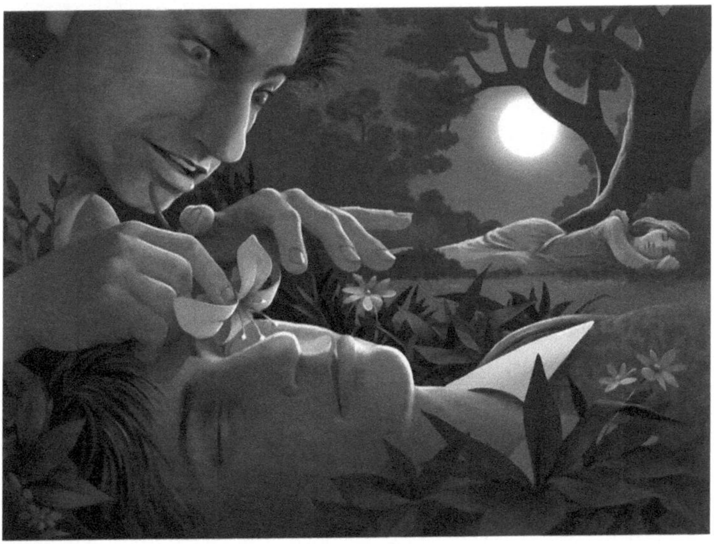

When you wake, you will fall in love! Now, I must go and find Oberon. *[Exit Puck]*

Puck: *Through the forest have I gone,*
But Athenian found I none,
On whose eyes I might approve
This flower's force in stirring love.
Night and silence: who is here?
Weeds of Athens he doth wear:
This is he (my master said)
Despised the Athenian maid:
And here the maiden sleeping sound,
On the dank and dirty ground.

approve = test
force = strength, power
stirring = mixing, making something happen
Night and silence = Goodness me!
weeds = clothes
doth = does
despised = hated
maid/maiden = young lady
sound = deeply
dank = cold and slightly wet

[Enter Demetrius and Helena, they are running]

Helena: Wait for me, Demetrius! Don't leave me in the dark.

Demetrius: Go away! Leave me alone! *[Demetrius leaves]*

Helena: *[Out of breath]* Oh, I cannot run any more. The more I wish for Demetrius's love, the more he hates me. Hermia is so lucky. He thinks she is beautiful, and he loves her. How did her eyes become so beautiful? I know it wasn't tears that made them so beautiful. My eyes have been washed with far more tears than hers. But I am as ugly as a bear. Even the wild animals that meet me run away scared. So it isn't surprising that Demetrius runs away from me like this too. Why did I ever think that he might love me? *[Suddenly sees Lysander asleep on the ground]* Who is this? It's Lysander! Is he dead or asleep? *[to Lysander]* Lysander, wake up! Wake up!

Lysander: *[Waking up]* Helena! Sweet Helena! I would run through fire for you! *[Angry]* Where is Demetrius? I want to kill him with my sword[41]!

Helena: Don't say that, Lysander. I know that he loves Hermia, but Hermia loves you, not him. So be happy

Lysander: Happy, with Hermia? No! I am sorry that I have wasted so much time with her. I don't love Hermia. I love you. Why would I love her instead of you? I didn't see things clearly before. But now, in your eyes, I see true love.

Lysander: *Where is Demetrius? O how fit a word*
Is that vile name to perish on my sword!
Helena: *Do not say so, Lysander, say not so.*
What though he love your Hermia? Lord, what though?
Yet Hermia still loves you; then be content.
Lysander: *Content with Hermia? No. I do repent*
The tedious minutes I with her have spent.
Not Hermia, but Helena I love:
Who will not change a raven for a dove?

fit = suitable, right
vile = horrible
perish = die
what though? = what does it matter?
content = happy
repent = regret, feel sorry about
tedious = long and boring
raven = a large ugly black bird
dove = a small beautiful white bird

Helena: Why are you making fun of[42] me like this? I have never treated you badly, so why are you doing this to me? Isn't it bad enough that Demetrius is not interested in me? And now, to make things worse, you make fun of me because I am not good enough for him. I thought you were a gentleman[43], Lysander. But I was wrong!

[Exit Helena]

Lysander: She did not see Hermia. *[Looking at Hermia, who is asleep]* Hermia, don't ever come near me again. I have had enough of you. I am like someone who has eaten too many sweet things. And all my love now is for Helena.

[Exit Lysander]

Hermia: *[Still asleep, screaming]* Help me, Lysander! Help me! A snake! *[Waking, to Lysander, who she believes is still there]* Oh, what an awful dream! I dreamed that a snake was eating away my heart, and you sat smiling as you watched it. *[Sitting up, and seeing that Lysander has gone]* Lysander, where are you? Lysander? Say something, if you can hear me! *[Waits for a moment]* Where has he gone? I feel sick with fear. I must find him at once or I will surely die.

[Hermia leaves]

Act 3, Scene 1

[Quince, Snug, Bottom and Flute meet in the wood. Titania is lying asleep to one side]

Bottom: Is everyone here?

Quince: Yes, we are all here. And this is a perfect place for us to rehearse our play.

Bottom: Peter Quince, there are some things in this play that people will not like. For example, Pyramus kills himself with his sword in the play. And the ladies will not like that at all.

Flute: Oh no, they will be very frightened!

Snug: Perhaps we should change the play, so that Pyramus does not kill himself.

Bottom: No, I have a better idea. Quince, you must write a prologue – a short introduction to the play. And in this prologue you must explain that we will not really hurt anyone with our swords, and that Pyramus does not really kill himself. And you should also say that I – Pyramus – am not Pyramus. I am in fact Bottom. And then no one will be frightened.

Quince: Good idea, Bottom. I shall do what you say, and write a prologue.

Snug: Do you think that the ladies will also be frightened of the lion?

Flute: Oh yes, I think they will!

Bottom: Gentlemen, it is terrible to bring a lion among ladies. The lion is the most frightening wild animal of all.

Flute: Then we must have another prologue. And this prologue should explain that the lion is not really a lion.

Bottom: No, I think there should be a hole in the lion's neck, so that people can see Snug's face through the hole.

And Snug should say: 'Fair ladies, please do not be afraid. Please don't think that I have come here as a lion. I am not a lion. I am a man.' And then Snug must tell everyone his name.

Quince: Right, we shall do that. *[Writing everything down]* But there is another problem. We need moonlight. In the story, Pyramus and Thisbe meet by moonlight.

Snug: Will the moon be shining on the night of the wedding?

Flute: Yes, it will.

Bottom: Well, then, you can leave a window open, and the moon will shine in.

Quince: Or someone could come in holding a light and he could say, 'This light shows the moon.' *[The other actors nod their heads and agree]* But there is another problem too. We need to have a wall, because in the story, Pyramus and Thisbe talked to each other through a hole in a wall.

Snug: Oh, you can't bring in a whole wall. What do you think, Bottom?

Bottom: Well, someone can pretend to be the wall. Someone can come in holding a stone, and say 'I am pretending to be the wall.' And he can hold his fingers like this to make a hole. *[Holds up two fingers in a V-shape]* And Pyramus and Thisbe can talk to each other through that hole.

Quince: Good! Everything is sorted, then. Sit down, everybody, and practise your parts. Pyramus, you begin. And when you have finished speaking, you have to leave. So you can go and stand behind that tree.

[Enter Puck. He stands to one side, watching the actors]

Puck: *[to himself]* Who are these simple townsmen? And

what are they doing so near to Titania's sleeping-place? Ah, they are rehearsing a play! I shall watch, and maybe take part[44] too. I shall have some fun here, I'm sure!

Quince: *[to Bottom]* Speak, Pyramus. *[to Flute]* Thisbe, come forward.

[Flute comes and stands near Bottom]

Bottom: *[as Pyramus]* Thisbe, the flowers smell so sweet, and so do you my dearest Thisbe, dear.

[Listening] I hear a voice! Stay here a moment, I will come back soon, do not fear.

[Bottom leaves. He goes and stands behind the tree]

Puck: *[to himself]* Yes, he will come back. But he will look very strange. *[Laughing]* Because I am going to give him a donkey's[45] head!

[Puck follows Bottom behind the tree]

Flute: Do I speak now, Quince?

Quince: Yes, you do. Pyramus has just gone to see what the noise was. He will be back soon.

Flute: *[as Thisbe]* Handsome Pyramus, you are as white as snow,

You are as red as roses, growing all around,

Oh, you are the loveliest young man I know,

Like a horse that never slows down.

I'll meet you later, Pyramus.

Quince: Stop, Flute! You don't say that yet. You say that after Pyramus has answered. Pyramus, come back! You are supposed to come back when you hear 'never slows down'.

[Bottom comes back, wearing a donkey's head. Puck follows him]

Bottom: *[as Pyramus]* I wish I could be yours, beautiful Thisbe.

[Quince, Snug and Flute see Bottom, with his donkey's head, and are terrified]

Quince: *[Shouting]* A strange animal! A monster[46]! Quick, everyone! Run! Help!

[Quince, Flute and Snug run away]

Puck: *[Laughing]* I'll follow these townsmen, and then I'll confuse them. Sometimes I'll pretend to be a horse, and sometimes I'll pretend to be a dog, or a bear. And I'll make them go round and round in circles.

[Exit Puck]

Bottom: *[Confused]* Why are they running away? Is this some silly joke? Are they trying to frighten me?

[Snug comes back]

Snug: *[Frightened]* Oh Bottom, what has happened to you?

Bottom: What are you talking about?

[Snug runs away, and Quince comes back]

Quince: Oh, poor Bottom. You have changed! It is terrible, terrible!

[Quince runs away]

Bottom: Oh, I understand their joke. They're trying to make a fool of[47] me and frighten me. Well, I'm not going to run away. I shall walk around right here, and I shall sing. Then they will hear me, and they will know that I am not afraid.

[Bottom sings]

Titania: *[Waking up]* What angel[48] wakes me from my flowery bed? *[Sees Bottom and looks at him, full of love]* Please, sir, sing again. It is wonderful to listen to you. And it is wonderful to look at you. In fact, there are many wonderful things about you. I think I have fallen in love with you at first sight[49].

Bottom: *[Surprised]* Oh, I don't think I'm the sort of man that people fall in love with. But then people often fall in love without thinking these days. And I must say, I can tell a very good joke.

Titania: So you are as clever as you are handsome.

Bottom: I don't really think so. I'm not even clever enough to find the way out of this wood.

Titania: Don't talk of leaving this wood! I will not let you go. I am a very important fairy, and I love you – so you must come with me. I will call some fairies to be your servants. They will sing to you while you sleep on a bed of flowers. And I will make you feel as light as a fairy. *[Calling]* Fairies!

Fairies: What can we do for you?

Titania: Be kind and polite to this gentleman. Dance for him, and feed him with fruit and honey. Light candles to take him to bed. And wave colourful butterfly wings over his sleepy eyes. Look after him, and bring him to my garden room.

[Exit all]

Act 3, Scene 2

[Oberon, King of the Fairies, comes in]

Oberon: I wonder if Titania is awake yet. And I wonder what the first thing she saw was when she woke up. Whatever it was, she must now be in love with it!

[Enter Puck]

Here comes Puck. Well, Puck? What has been happening in the wood?

Puck: *[Laughing]* Titania is in love with a monster! While she was asleep, a group of foolish[50] craftsmen from Athens were rehearsing a play near her sleeping place. The most foolish one was playing the part of Pyramus. And when he walked away into the trees during the play, I put a donkey's head on him! When the other craftsmen saw him with the donkey's head, they ran away like frightened animals! They were terrified, and I led them round and round the wood. But Pyramus stayed. And at that moment, Titania woke up, and immediately fell in love with a donkey-man!

Oberon: *[Laughing]* This is better than I had hoped! But have you found the Athenian and put love juice in his eyes?

Puck: Yes, I found him sleeping, with the Athenian lady by his side. I was sure that when he woke up, he would see her straight away.

[Enter Demetrius and Hermia]

Oberon: Hide, Puck! Here is the same Athenian.

Puck: That is the woman that I saw. But it is not the man whose eyes I put love juice on.

[Oberon and Puck move away]

Demetrius: Why are you so angry with me, when I love you? You should save your anger for the people who hate you!

Hermia: If I am right about what you have done, I am going to be much angrier than this. I believe that you killed Lysander while he was asleep. Did you? Did you? *[Demetrius shakes his head, confused]* Lysander was more faithful[51] to me than the sun is to the day. He would never have left me while I was sleeping. I am sure that you have murdered[52] him! You look like a murderer: you look full of death. Go on, murderer. Why don't you go a bit further, and kill me too?

Demetrius: You are wasting your anger on me. I did not kill Lysander. And he is not dead, as far as I know.

Hermia: Please tell me, then, that he is well.

Demetrius: If I could tell you that, what would you give me?

Hermia: I would give you a promise: you will never see me again. Anyway, enough of this! I am going. And I never want to see you again, even if Lysander is still alive.

[Exit Hermia]

Demetrius: *[to himself]* I am not going to follow her, when she is angry like this. My heart feels full of sadness. And I am tired. That makes the sadness even stronger. So I will rest here for a while. *[Demetrius lies down and sleeps. Oberon and Puck come forward]*

Oberon: *[to Puck]* What have you done? You have put love juice in the wrong person's eyes! And now, instead of bringing two hearts together, you have broken two apart! Go quicker than the wind, and find Helena of Athens. She is love-sick, and full of sadness. Bring her here. I shall put some love juice in Demetrius's eyes, ready for when she comes.

Puck: I shall go as fast as an arrow[53] of love.

[Exit Puck]

Oberon: *[Squeezing love juice in Demetrius's eyes]* Juice from this purple flower, go deep into his eyes. When he sees Helena, let her shine as brightly as the stars in the sky. When he wakes up, if she is there, let him beg[54] for her love.

[Enter Puck]

Puck: My lord, Helena is coming! And she is with the man that I saw earlier. He is the one that I gave the love juice to by mistake. He is begging her for her love! Shall we watch them? It will probably be very funny! These people who live in the real world are such fools! *[Sound of people arguing]*

Oberon: Stand over here. The noise they are making will wake Demetrius up.

Puck: Then two men will be begging Helena for her love! That really will be funny. *[Laughing]* This is just the sort of thing that I enjoy!

[Oberon and Puck stand to one side; Enter Lysander and Helena]

Lysander: *[to Helena]* Why won't you believe that I love you? Why do you think that I am mocking[55] you? People never mock with tears. And look how I cry every time I tell you that I love you. Those tears should show you that I am telling the truth[56].

Helena: Those tears show me that you are clever at getting what you want! You told Hermia that you loved her. So if you are telling the truth now, then you have lied to her. And if you were telling her the truth, then you are lying to me.

Lysander: I was not thinking properly when I told Hermia that I loved her.

Helena: And you are not thinking properly now, either, when you tell me that you do not love her anymore.

Lysander: Demetrius loves Hermia. He doesn't love you.

Demetrius: *[Waking up]* Oh Helena, you are perfect! You are beautiful! Your eyes are clearer than crystal[57]. Your lips are like red cherries, waiting to be kissed. Your hands are whiter than snow. Let me kiss your hand and I shall be happy for ever.

Helena: I do not believe this! I see that you have both decided to make fun of me for your own enjoyment. If you were proper gentlemen, you would never treat me like this. Suddenly you tell me that you love me, and make promises to me. But I know that you both hate me. So why don't you just treat me like someone that you hate? Why do you have to mock me like this? You have both been fighting for Hermia's love. And now you are fighting to make fun of me!

Helena: *If you were civil, and knew courtesy,*
You would not do me this much injury.
Can you not hate me, as I know you do,
But you must join in souls to mock me too?
If you were men, as men you are in show,
You would not use a gentle lady so:
To vow, and swear, and superpraise my parts,
When I am sure you hate me with your hearts.
You both are rivals, and love Hermia;
And now both rivals to mock Helena.

civil = polite
courtesy = good manners
injury = harm, when someone hurts you
join in souls = get together
in show = in appearance, looking like
vow, swear = make promises
superpraise = say lots of very good things about
rivals = people who want the same thing

Lysander: You are being unkind, Demetrius. You love Hermia. We all know that. So let's make an agreement[58]. Hermia gave her heart to me, and I now give that to you. And in return, you must give me Helena's heart, which she gave to you. For I love Helena, and I shall love her until I die.

Demetrius: Lysander, keep your Hermia. If ever I felt love for her, that love is now gone. I was not thinking properly for a while. But now my heart is Helena's once more. And it will always be Helena's.

Lysander: Do not believe him, Helena.

Demetrius: *[to Lysander]* If you talk in that way, I will make you sorry for it. *[Sees Hermia coming]* Look, here's your love, coming now.

[Enter Hermia]

Hermia: Lysander? I could not see you in the darkness, but I heard your voice. Why did you leave me, Lysander?

Lysander: How could I stay with you when love was calling me away?

Hermia: What love could take you away from me?

Lysander: My love for Helena, who shines more brightly than all the stars. Why did you come looking for me? Didn't you realize[59] that I left you because I hate you?

Hermia: *[Confused]* You can't be thinking properly. This can't be true!

Helena: *[Angry]* So she is part of this joke, as well! The three of you have got together to make fun of me. *[to Hermia]* How can you do this to me, Hermia? We were best friends! We were like sisters! Have you forgotten that? We used to do everything together. We were like two cherries hanging from the same stem[60], we were two people with the same heart. And now you are happy to throw away that friendship so that you can make fun of me with these men. Women should not treat each other like this!

Hermia: I don't understand what you are saying! I am not making fun of you. It seems that you are making fun of me!

Helena: You sent Lysander to follow me and tell me that he loves me. And then you sent Demetrius, your other love, as well. Just a short time ago, he was running away from me. And now he tells me that I am perfect and beautiful. Why would he talk like that to someone that he hates? Lysander loves you. But he pretends that he hates you, and loves me instead. Why would he do that? You must have told him to! You are so lucky – two men love you. But the man I love does not care for me. You should feel sorry for me! You shouldn't make fun of me.

Hermia: What are you talking about? I don't understand.

Helena: Oh yes, go on! Keep that sad face! Then laugh at me when I turn my back! If you knew how to behave nicely, you would not make fun of me like this. I'm going to go now. At least when I have gone, or when I am dead, you will not be able to treat me this way!

Lysander: *[Holding her back]* Wait! Listen to me. You are my love, my life, fair Helena!

Helena: *[Angry]* Oh, I don't believe this!

Hermia: Don't make fun of her like this, sweet Lysander.

Lysander: *[to Hermia]* Leave me alone. *[to Helena]* Helena, I love you. I will fight any man who says that I do not love you – and I will happily die for you.

Demetrius: *[to Helena]* I love you more than he does.

Lysander: *[to Demetrius]* Then let's go and fight! Prove[61] that you really love her!

Hermia: *[Trying to hold Lysander back]* What is this all about, Lysander? What has happened to you, my sweet love?

Lysander: *[Trying to push her away]* Get away from me! You are like something horrible that I have been made to drink.

Hermia: You can't mean these things that you are saying. You must be joking.

Helena: *[Still thinking that they are joking]* Of course he does. And so do you.

Demetrius: *[to Lysander]* Come on, you coward[62]. Are you going to let a woman stop you?

Lysander: What am I supposed to do? Hit her, kill her? Although I hate her, I won't hurt her.

Hermia: *[Suddenly realizing that Lysander means what he says]* Hate me? You can't hurt me any more than that! Why do you hate me? Aren't I Hermia? Aren't you Lysander? I am as fair now as I was yesterday. Tonight you loved me, and tonight you left me. Then is it really true? Did you really want to leave me?

Lysander: Yes, and I never want to see you again. I am telling you the truth. This is not a joke. I hate you. And I love Helena.

Hermia: *[Crying out]* What? *[to Helena]* You love-thief[63]! You cheat[64]! You have come in the night and stolen my love's heart from him!

Helena: *[Angry]* Haven't you gone far enough already with this joke? Now you are trying to argue with me! You liar! You puppet[65], you!

Hermia: 'Puppet'? That's what you call me now, is it? Suddenly you think it is important that you are taller than me. Is that how you stole Lysander from me? Well, I am not as short as you think! I am still tall enough to reach your eyes with my nails!

Helena: Gentlemen, mock me if you must, but please don't let her hurt me. I have never been good at arguing. And just because she is shorter than me, it doesn't mean that I am better at fighting.

Hermia: Shorter? There she goes again!

Helena: Good Hermia, don't be so angry with me. I have always loved you. I have always kept your secrets, and I have never done anything to hurt you. Except that, because of my love for Demetrius, I told him that you were running away with Lysander. He followed you, and I, for love, followed him. But he sent me away. He told me that he would hurt me, or even kill me. So please let me go now, and I will return to Athens and leave you alone. I am just a simple girl. Let me go. *[She waits]*

Hermia: Go on, then! What's stopping you?

Helena: My foolish heart, which is still in love.

Hermia: *[Angry again]* With Lysander?

Helena: No, with Demetrius.

Lysander: Don't be afraid. I won't let her hurt you, Helena.

Helena: Oh, when she is angry, she is so cold and hard. She is only little, but she is so fierce[66].

Hermia: 'Little' again? Why do you let her talk to me like this? Let me get at her! *[Pushing forward towards Helena]*

Lysander: *[Holding her back]* Get off, you puppet, you acorn.

Demetrius: *[to Lysander]* Helena does not want your help. Leave her alone, or you will be sorry.

Lysander: Follow me, if you are brave enough, and we shall fight for Helena's love.

Demetrius: Follow you? No, I'll go with you side by side.

[Exit Lysander and Demetrius]

Hermia: *[to Helena]* This is all your fault. *[Helena starts to walk away]* Don't leave.

Helena: I don't trust you, and I don't want to stay here with you. You are better at fighting than me, but I am quicker at running away.

[Exit Helena]

Hermia: I am amazed[67]. I don't know what to say.

[Exit Hermia. Oberon and Puck come forward]

Oberon: This is your fault. Did you cause this mischief on purpose[68]?

Puck: Believe me, King of the Fairies, I made a mistake. You told me to find an Athenian and put the love juice in his eyes. And that's what I did! I do find it funny to watch these lovers' arguments!

Oberon: Demetrius and Lysander are looking for a place to fight. Go then, Puck, and make the night dark. Cover the starry sky with fog, so that it is as black as the darkest river. And make these lovers get lost, so that they cannot find each other. Pretend to be first Lysander, and then Demetrius. Lead them away from each other, until they are too tired to go on. Then put the juice of this flower in Lysander's eyes. It will break the love spell, and make him see clearly again. And he will love the right person once more. When these lovers all wake up, this night will seem like a dream. And they will go back to Athens and stay friends until they die. While you are doing this, I shall go and find my queen. I shall ask her for her little boy. And then I shall break the spell, and stop her being in love with that monster. And everything will be peaceful once more.

Oberon: *[to Puck] When they next wake, all this derision*
Shall seem a dream and fruitless vision;
And back to Athens shall the lovers wend,
With league whose date till death shall never end.
Whiles I in this affair do thee employ,
I'll to my queen, and beg her Indian boy;

And then I will her charmed eye release
From monster's view, and all things shall be peace.

derision = mockery
fruitless = something that does not give results
vision = a dream, something you see that is not real
wend = go
league = friendship
affair = situation
thee = you (Puck)
employ = give someone a job, get someone working
charmed = under a spell
release = let go

Puck: My fairy lord, we must be quick. Dawn is coming. The morning star is already shining, and the night ghosts[69] are returning home.

Oberon: Yes, we should try and do these things before morning.

[Exit Oberon]

Puck: *[Singing]* Up and down, up and down,
I will lead them up and down;
People are afraid of me, in country and in town:
Fairy, lead them up and down.
Here comes one of the lovers.

[Enter Lysander]

Lysander: *[Looking around in the darkness and calling out loudly]* Where are you, proud Demetrius? Speak now!

Puck: *[Talking in Demetrius's voice]* I am here, and my sword is ready. Follow me!

[Exit Lysander, following the voice. Enter Demetrius, stabbing[70] his sword at the bushes in the darkness]

Demetrius: *[Calling out loudly]* Lysander, speak. Have you run away, coward? Where are you hiding?

Puck: *[Talking in Lysander's voice]* You coward! You tell the bushes that you are ready to fight, but you don't come forward. Come out of the bushes, little boy! I shall hit you with a stick. It wouldn't be right to fight you with a sword. Follow me!

[Exit Demetrius and Puck. Enter Lysander]

Lysander: He tells me to follow, but whenever I go after him he has already disappeared. He is much faster than me, and the ground here is not good. I shall rest here. *[He lies down]* Come, gentle day. As soon as I see your grey light, I shall find Demetrius. And I shall make him sorry for running away.

[Lysander sleeps. Enter Puck and Demetrius]

Puck: *[Talking in Lysander's voice, and laughing]* Come on, coward! What are you waiting for? *[They move around, and Demetrius stabs his sword at the air, because he cannot see Puck]*

Demetrius: Wait for me if you are brave enough. I know very well that you are running away and hiding. You aren't brave enough to stand still and look me in the face. Where are you now?

Puck: Come on! I am here.

Demetrius: You are mocking me. You will be sorry for this, if I find you in the morning. Go on! I am tired, and I am going to lie down here on the cold grass. *[He lies down]* I shall come and find you at dawn.

[He sleeps. Enter Helena]

Helena: Oh, this night is going on for ever! When will the sun come up? I want to go back to Athens by daylight, and get away from these people who hate me. Sleep helps us to escape from our sadness. Come, sleep, and take me away from myself for a while.

[She lies down and sleeps]

Puck: That's three of the lovers. We just need one more now. *[Sees Hermia coming]* Ah, here she comes, so angry and sad. Love is unkind, playing tricks[71] on these poor women!

[Enter Hermia]

Hermia: I have never felt so tired, or so full of sadness. I can go no further. I shall rest here until morning.

[She lies down]

I pray that Lysander will be safe, if he and Demetrius fight.

[She sleeps]

Puck: Sleep well, there on the ground. And I shall break the love spell with this flower. *[He squeezes juice in Lysander's eyes]* When you wake, you will once again love the lady you loved before. And then everyone will be happy.

[Exit Puck]

Act 4, Scene 1

[Lysander, Demetrius, Helena and Hermia are still asleep, to one side. Enter Titania and her fairies, with Bottom. Oberon is standing behind, where no one can see him]

Titania: *[to Bottom]* Come and sit down on this flowery bed, and let me gently touch your cheeks. Let me put sweet-smelling roses all around your head, and kiss your large ears, my love.

Bottom: Where are the fairies?

Fairies: We're here.

Bottom: Bring me some honey, please, fairies. And scratch[72] my head. My face feels very hairy. And as soon as I get a bit hairy, I just have to scratch.

Titania: Would you like to have some music, my sweet love?

Bottom: Oh yes, I have a very good ear for music. Let's have clappers and triangles[73]!

Titania: *[Looks rather surprised and quickly thinks of something else to say]* And what would you like to eat, sweet love?

Bottom: You know, some nice dry oats and hay[74] would be lovely. Good sweet hay: there's nothing like it! *[He yawns]* But please let me just lie down for a while. I'm suddenly feeling very tired.

Titania: Sleep then, and I shall hold you in my arms. Fairies, off you go!

[The fairies leave]

[Titania puts her arms around Bottom]

I shall wrap myself around you like ivy[75] around a tree. Oh, how I love you!

[They sleep]

[Enter Puck]

Oberon: *[Coming forward]* Hello, Puck. Do you see Titania and the donkey-man lying there? *[He points at them]* I feel rather sorry for Titania now. When I met her earlier, she was picking flowers and putting them around that fool's hairy head. There were dewdrops on the flowers, and it was as if they were crying tears of shame[76]. I told her she was being foolish, and argued with her. And then I asked her to give me her little boy. And she immediately promised him to me and sent him off to Fairy Land. Now I have the boy, I shall break this hateful love spell. Puck, take the donkey's head off this Athenian. When he wakes up, he and the others will all go back to Athens. And they will believe that this night has just been a dream. But first let me set the fairy queen free.

[Oberon squeezes juice into Titania's eyes]

Be as you used to be,
See as you used to see,
This pretty flower has a sweet juice
Which has a very special use.
Now my Titania, wake up, sweet queen.

Titania: *[Waking up]* My Oberon! I have had the strangest dream! I thought I was in love with a donkey.

Oberon: *[Pointing at Bottom]* There he is.

Titania: *[Shocked]* How did this happen? I hate to look at him now.

Oberon: Be quiet for a moment. Puck, take off the donkey-head. Titania, call for music. *[He points at Bottom and the four lovers]* Let these five sleep more deeply than the sleep of death.

Titania: Fairies, music! Play music that will bring sleep. *[Gentle music starts playing quietly]*

Puck: *[Taking the donkey-head off Bottom]* Now when you wake up, you will see with your own fool's eyes!

Oberon: Let the music play more loudly! *[The music plays a dance]*

Come, my queen, take my hand, and let's dance around these sleeping lovers. *[Oberon and Titania dance]* We are friends again, and tomorrow night we shall dance together at Duke Theseus's house, and bless his marriage. These four lovers will be married there with Theseus, and everyone will be happy again.

Oberon: *Come my queen, take hands with me,*
And rock the ground whereon these sleepers be.
[Oberon and Titania dance]
Now thou and I are new in amity,
And will to-morrow midnight, solemnly,
Dance in Duke Theseus' house triumphantly,
And bless it to all fair prosperity.
There shall the pairs of faithful lovers be
Wedded, with Theseus, all in jollity.

thou = you
amity = friendship
solemnly = seriously, for an important occasion
triumphantly = full of excitement and pleasure
prosperity = being successful and having plenty of money
wedded = married
jollity = happiness

Puck: My fairy king, listen! I hear the morning birds.

Oberon: Then, my queen, let us silently follow the darkness of the night. We shall go around the world more quickly than the moon.

Titania: Come, my lord. And as we go, tell me why I was sleeping on the ground with these people from the real world.

[Exit Puck, Oberon and Titania. The four lovers and Bottom are still asleep]

[Enter Theseus, Hippolyta, Egeus and their attendants[77]*. There is a sound of horns*[78]*]*

Theseus: Well, it is a beautiful morning for hunting[79]. *[to Hippolyta]* My love, when my hunting-dogs run across the valley, you will hear the sound of their music. *[to an attendant]* Let the dogs go! *[to Hippolyta]* Let's go up to the top of the mountain, my fair queen, and listen to them there. *[Suddenly sees the lovers lying on the ground.]* But wait, who are these young people? Go quietly, everyone!

Egeus: *[Pointing at the lovers]* My lord, this is my daughter, asleep. And this is Lysander. This is Demetrius, and this is Helena. What are they all doing here?

Theseus: Perhaps they heard that we were coming here, and got up early to see us. *[Suddenly remembers something]* Egeus, hasn't Hermia promised to tell us her choice today?

Egeus: She has, my lord.

Theseus: *[to his attendants]* Wake them up with the horns!

[Sound of horns. The lovers wake and sit up]

Good morning, my friends!

[The lovers see Theseus and bow down]

Stand up, please. Lysander, you and Demetrius hate each other. Why are you lying here peacefully, side by side?

Lysander: My lord, I am only half awake. I think – no, I am sure – that I came to this wood with Hermia. We wanted to get away from Athens. We wanted to escape from the laws of the city so that we could . . .

Egeus: *[to Theseus]* That is enough, my lord. He has tried to break the law of Athens. Demetrius, they were trying to run away. I had promised you that my daughter would be your wife. And they were trying to cheat us both.

Demetrius: My lord, fair Helena told me that they were running away to this wood. Full of anger, I followed them here, and Helena, for love, followed me. But, my good lord, something strange has happened. My love for Hermia has melted[80] like the snow. And now I can only think about Helena. I was in love with her before I met Hermia. But, like a sick man who starts to hate his food, I turned against her. And now I feel like someone who is well again and can eat once more! And I want Helena. I love her, I need her, and I will always be faithful to her!

Theseus: Young lovers, it is lucky that you all met like this. We'll hear more about this later. Egeus, I will not bring the law of Athens against your daughter. Instead, these young lovers will be married at the temple[81], together with us. It is too late to go hunting now. Let's all return to Athens, and celebrate this important day together. Come on, Hippolyta.

[Exit Theseus, Hippolyta, Egeus and their attendants]

Demetrius: I can hardly remember what happened last night. Nothing is clear. It is as if mountains that were a long way away have now turned into clouds.

Hermia: Yes, I cannot think clearly at all.

Helena: Nor can I. And I feel as if Demetrius is mine, but not mine. It is like finding something very important. It is mine because I have found it, but it belongs to someone else.

Demetrius: Are you sure that we are awake? Perhaps we are still sleeping, and this is all a dream. Am I imagining it, or was the Duke here? And didn't he tell us to go with him?

Hermia: Yes, the Duke was here – and so was my father.

Helena: And Hippolyta.

Lysander: And he told us to go with him to the temple.

Demetrius: Then we must be awake. Let's go with him, and let's tell each other about our dreams on the way there.

Demetrius: *Are you sure*
That we are awake? It seems to me
That yet we sleep, we dream. Do not you think
The Duke was here, and bid us follow him?
Hermia: *Yea, and my father.*
Helena: *And Hippolyta.*
Lysander: *And he did bid us follow to the temple.*
Demetrius: *Why then, we are awake: let's follow him,*
And by the way let us recount our dreams.

yet = still
bid = told (us) to
yea = yes
by the way = on the way
recount = tell

[Exit Lysander and Demetrius]

Bottom: *[Talking in his sleep]* Tell me when I have to speak again. I have to wait until I hear the line 'Most fair Pyramus.' *[Yawns, and then suddenly wakes up]* Peter Quince? Where are you? Flute? Snug? Well, I don't believe it! They've gone away and left me sleeping. I have had a very strange dream. Very strange. I thought I was . . . *[Laughing]* and I thought I had . . . *[Laughing again]*. Yes, what a strange dream! I shall ask Peter Quince to write a song about this dream. And it will be called 'Bottom's Dream', because it has no bottom! Perhaps I'll sing it when we perform the play for the Duke. Yes, I'll sing it at the end, when Thisbe dies.

[Exit Bottom]

Act 4, Scene 2

[Enter Quince and Flute]

Quince: Did you send someone to look for Bottom at his house? Has he come home yet?

Flute: No. No one knows where he is. Someone has taken him away, I'm sure! They have turned him into a donkey-man and taken him away! What shall we do if we can't find him? We won't be able to perform the play without him, will we?

Quince: Definitely not. There is no one in Athens who can play Pyramus as well as Bottom.

Flute: No, he is the cleverest craftsman in the city.

Quince: He is a fine-looking man, too. And he has a wonderful voice.

[Enter Snug]

Snug: Gentlemen, the Duke is on his way back from the temple. And two other ladies and gentlemen have been married there, too. I'm sure they will pay anyone who performs for them very well. If we were able to do the play we could be rich men!

Flute: Poor dear old Bottom. He could have made so much money – but instead he has been taken away!

[Enter Bottom]

Bottom: Where are my old friends?

Quince: *[Very excited]* Bottom! Oh, happy day!

Bottom: Gentlemen, I have some amazing things to tell you. But don't ask me what they are. I can't possibly tell you.

Quince: Do tell us, sweet Bottom.

Bottom: No, no, I shan't say a word about that. But I can tell you that the Duke has had dinner. His celebrations will begin soon. Get your clothes ready, tidy up your beards and shine your shoes. And let's meet at the palace. For the Duke's attendant has chosen several plays for tonight's celebrations. And one of them is ours! *[Flute, Snug and Quince cheer]* Thisbe, put on your clean underwear! *[Flute, Snug and Quince laugh]* Lion, don't cut your nails – they must be sharp tonight! *[Flute, Snug and Quince laugh again]* And don't go eating onions, my friends. We need to have sweet breath. Now, go, everyone!

[Exit all]

Act 5, Scene 1

[The Duke's palace in Athens: Enter Theseus and Hippolyta, with their attendants]

Hippolyta: The things these lovers have been talking about are very strange, my Theseus.

Theseus: They are strange, but they are probably not true. I never believe strange stories like these, or silly talk about fairies. Lovers' heads are so full of dreams, they always think up incredible stories. A sensible[82] person could never believe their stories.

Hippolyta: But when I heard them tell the whole story, it seemed like more than just young lovers' dreams. The way they were feeling changed so suddenly, and at the same time! Anyway, it was certainly a very strange story.

[Enter Hermia, Lysander, Demetrius and Helena]

Theseus: Here come the lovers, full of happiness! Now, gentle friends, there are still three hours until bedtime. How shall we pass the time? What entertainment[83] and dances shall we have? *[Turns to one of his attendants]* Is there a play that we could watch?

Attendant: *[Comes forward, holding a paper]* Here is a list of the plays that are ready for you to see, my lord. *[Gives Theseus the paper]* Which one would you like to see first?

Theseus: *[Reading the list]* Well, this one is an old one, that I have already seen. And this one is not really suitable for a wedding celebration. *[Laughs]* Now, this one sounds interesting! *[Reads]* 'A tedious[84] short play about young Pyramus and his love Thisbe – a happy tragedy[85].' Tedious and short? A happy tragedy? It is like hot snow! How can we make sense[86] of this nonsense?

Attendant: It is the shortest play that I have ever seen, my lord. And yet it is still too long and tedious. There is not one sensible word in the play, or one good actor. The play is a tragedy. Pyramus kills himself, which is terribly sad. And when I saw the actors rehearsing this part, I cried. But I'm afraid that my tears were tears of laughter!

Theseus: *[Laughing]* Who are the actors?

Attendant: They are craftsmen from Athens. They are used to working with their hands, not their heads. And they are not used to learning plays. But they have rehearsed this one specially for your wedding celebrations.

Theseus: And we shall see it.

Attendant: No, my lord. You will not enjoy it. It is no good at all. Although you may find it quite funny to watch them try and perform it. It is certainly not easy for them: they have worked painfully hard to try and please you.

Theseus: I would like to see that play, then. If they are simply trying to please us, that is all that matters. Go and bring the actors in. Ladies, take your seats.

[Exit attendant]

Hippolyta: *[to Theseus]* Is this really a good idea? I don't like to see people making fools of themselves, and trying too hard.

Theseus: The important thing is not the play itself. The important thing is that they are trying to please us. When I travel around, I sometimes meet very clever people, who have obviously spent a long time rehearsing a speech[87] for me. But when they see me, they turn pale, and forget what they were going to say. Other people give perfect speeches. They are not afraid to speak to a duke. But believe me, the ones who are silent are just as important to me. Their nervous silence shows that they have great respect[88] for me.

[Enter the attendant]

Attendant: My lord, the actors are ready.

Theseus: Then let the play begin!

[Trumpets[89] play. Enter Quince]

Quince: *[as prologue]* Ladies and gentlemen, here is the prologue. We hope that our play will upset you. *[Starts again]* Er, I mean, we hope that our play will not upset you. We have not come here to please you. *[Starts again]* Sorry, I mean, we have come here to please you. The actors are here, and they will show you everything you need to know.

Theseus: He tells his story in a very simple way and he is not sure whether we should be upset or pleased!

Hippolyta: Yes, he is like a child playing a musical instrument. You can hear something, but it is rather mixed up!

[Enter Bottom as Pyramus, Flute as Thisbe, and Snug as Lion]

Quince: *[as Prologue]* Ladies and gentlemen, this man is Pyramus, *[Bottom comes forward]* and this beautiful lady is Thisbe. *[Flute comes forward]* And I am the wall. *[He picks up a large stone]* I am the hateful wall which kept these lovers apart. And this *[He picks up a light]* is the moon. The lovers met at the temple by moonlight. And this is Lion *[Snug comes forward]* who frightened Thisbe away when she arrived at the temple. As she ran away, she dropped her mantle[90]. And the lion, which had a bloody mouth, marked[91] the mantle with blood. Then Pyramus came along, and found Thisbe's mantle covered with blood. He pulled out his sword and killed himself. And Thisbe, who was waiting nearby, took the sword and killed herself too. Lion, myself (the wall) and the lovers will explain the rest of the story to you.

[Exit Pyramus, Thisbe and Lion]

Theseus: Do you think the lion will speak?

Demetrius: I wouldn't be surprised, my lord. Even a lion could not be more foolish than this man!

Quince: In this play, before you all,
I am here to show you the wall,
Through which the lovers, Pyramus and Thisbe,
Often talked, very secretly.
And this stone *[Holds up the stone]* is here to show
That I am the wall. So now you know.
And here is the hole *[Holds up two fingers in a V-shape]* through which the lovers
Talked quietly to one another.

Theseus: *[Laughing]* I have never heard a wall speak so well before.

Demetrius: It is the cleverest wall that I have ever heard, my lord!

[Enter Bottom as Pyramus]

Bottom: *[as Pyramus]* Oh wall! O sweet and lovely wall!
Has Thisbe forgotten her promise?
Why doesn't she come when I call?
Show me your hole! *[Wall holds his fingers up in a V-shape]* Thank you for this!
[Looks through the hole] I cannot see Thisbe. Where can she be?
Oh hateful wall. Why do you stop her from being with me?

Theseus: The wall is very clever. It probably doesn't like it when Pyramus talks like this. Perhaps the wall should argue with him.

Bottom: *[Coming forward to talk to the duke]* No, my lord, the wall doesn't argue. When Thisbe hears the words 'stop her

from being with me', she speaks. She will come in now, and I will see her through the wall. Yes, look: here she comes.

[Enter Flute as Thisbe]

Flute: *[as Thisbe]* Oh Wall, I am so sad. Can't you see?
You keep Pyramus away from me.

Bottom: *[as Pyramus]* I hear a voice! Oh hole, let me see the sweet face of my Thisbe. *[Looks through the hole]* Thisbe!

Flute: *[as Thisbe]* My love! You are my love, I think.

Bottom: *[as Pyramus]* Thisbe, my love will always be true.

Flute: *[as Thisbe]* And mine, dear Pyramus, for you too.

Bottom: *[as Pyramus]* Kiss me through this hateful wall.

[Thisbe and Pyramus try to kiss through the hole]

Flute: *[as Thisbe]* I kiss the hole, not your lips at all.

Bottom: *[as Pyramus]* Will you meet me at the temple, just you and me?

Flute: *[as Thisbe]* I promise I'll go there immediately.

[Pyramus and Thisbe leave, separately]

Snug: *[as the Wall]* I, Wall, have played my part so. And now it is done, away I go.

[Wall leaves]

Hippolyta: This is the silliest play I have ever seen!

Theseus: Well, I think the actors believe that they are rather good. Ah, here comes the lion, with the moon.

[Enter the lion, carrying a light]

Snug: *[as Lion]* Ladies, I know that your gentle hearts fear
The smallest mouse that runs across the floor.
And so you will be very frightened here
When the lion lets out an angry roar.
So please remember, I am not a lion but a man,

My name is Snug, and I am a craftsman.
You can also see that I am holding a light.
And that is the moon, which shines so bright.

Theseus: I have never seen such a gentle lion!

Demetrius: No, my lord. And I have never seen such a terrible actor!

Theseus: Be quiet, everyone. Here comes Thisbe!

[Enter Flute as Thisbe]

Flute: *[as Thisbe]* This is the temple. Where is my love!

[The lion roars. Thisbe drops her mantle and runs away]

Demetrius: Well roared, lion!

Theseus: Well run, Thisbe!

Hippolyta: Well shone, moon!

[The lion pushes at the mantle with its mouth, and then leaves]

[Enter Bottom as Pyramus. He picks up the mantle, looking very upset]

Bottom: *[as Pyramus]* What terrible sadness is here?
Eyes, do you see?
How can it be?
Oh my Thisbe, my dear!
Your mantle's in the mud,
All covered in blood!
A lion has taken my love! Oh my!
Here where it roared
I take my sword,
And now I die, die, die, die, die! *[Pyramus stabs himself with his sword and dies]*

[Enter Thisbe as Flute, and sees Pyramus on the ground]

Flute: *[as Thisbe]* Asleep, my love?
[Looks at him more closely]
What, dead, my dove?
O Pyramus, why did you have to die?
[Sees Pyramus's sword and picks it up]
Then goodbye, my friends
Thisbe too must end
Goodbye, goodbye, goodbye! *[Thisbe stabs herself with Pyramus's sword and dies]*

Theseus: So poor Lion has to take away the dead bodies!

Demetrius: Yes, and Wall.

Bottom: *[Sitting up]* No, my lord. After Pyramus and Thisbe die, the wall is taken down. Now, we have rehearsed a short epilogue[92]. Would you like to see the epilogue, or dance?

Theseus: Oh, no. No epilogue, please. That was a very great tragedy. And I shall always remember it. But the play was long enough. Let us have a short dance!

[The craftsmen dance, and then leave]

It is midnight. Lovers, we must go to bed. I think we will all sleep late tomorrow. This play made us laugh so much that the evening has gone very quickly. Go to bed, sweet friends. We will be celebrating for the next two weeks.

[Exit all]

[Enter Puck]

Puck: The hungry lion is roaring, and the night ghosts are coming out. And now we fairies, who hide away from the sun and follow darkness like a dream, are ready to dance. But first I have come to sweep[93] the house and make it clean.

[Puck starts sweeping]

[Enter Oberon and Titania, with their fairies]

Oberon: Fairies, light the house with candles. And then come and sing and dance with us. *[The fairies light candles and move into a big circle]*

Titania: Let us hold hands, and sing, and bless this place.

[The fairies follow Oberon, singing and dancing]

Oberon: *Through the house give glimmering light*
By the dead and drowsy fire;
Every elf and fairy sprite
Hop as light as bird from briar;

And this ditty after me
Sing, and dance it trippingly.
Titania: *First rehearse your song by rote,*
To each word a warbling note;
Hand in hand, with fairy grace,
Will we sing, and bless this place.

glimmering = shining with a very small light that goes on and off
drowsy = sleepy
elf, sprite = magic fairy-like creatures
briar = rosebush
ditty = song
trippingly = quickly and lightly
by rote = by saying it many times
warbling = singing in a high voice, that moves up and down very quickly, like a birdsong
grace = beautiful way of moving

Oberon: Now, fairies, go to every room in the house. Titania and I will go and bless Theseus's bed. Take these special dewdrops *[Gives them out to the fairies]* and go all over the palace, blessing it with sweet peace. We must work through the night. We will bless this house so that these three couples will always be faithful to each other. And they will always be safe and happy. Off you go! Meet me here at dawn.

[Exit all except Puck]

Puck: *[to the audience]* If we fairies have upset you, just imagine that you have been sleeping here, and that this has all been a dream. If you can forgive us, we will try to do better next time. So goodnight to you all. Give us some applause[94], if we are still friends!

[Exit Puck]

Points for Understanding

Act 1

1 Why was Egeus angry with Hermia and Lysander?
2 What did Theseus say would happen to Hermia if she did not marry Demetrius?
3 Lysander asked Hermia to meet him in a wood outside Athens. Why?
4 Why did Demetrius stop loving Helena?
5 What play were the craftsmen rehearsing?
6 What parts did everyone have in the play?

Act 2

1 What had Oberon and Titania had an argument about?
2 At the beginning of Scene 1, how did the fairy describe Puck? What examples did she give of the way he behaves?
3 Why didn't Titania want to give the little boy to Oberon?
4 Oberon asked Puck to go and get a special purple flower. What was special about the flower?
5 Why did Demetrius come to the palace wood?
6 Oberon and Puck both put the juice of the purple flower on someone's eyes. Whose eyes did they put it on?
7 What was strange about the way Lysander spoke to Helena when he woke up?

Act 3

1 Why were Quince, Snug and Flute so frightened when they saw Bottom?
2 What did Titania fall in love with when she woke up?
3 What mistake had Puck made with the love juice?
4 What did Oberon and Puck do to try and make things right?

5 Why did Helena think that Lysander and Demetrius were making fun of her?
6 Why was Hermia angry with Helena?
7 Why did Lysander and Demetrius want to fight?
8 How did Puck stop them from fighting?
9 Puck put more juice into Lysander's eyes when he fell asleep. Why?

Act 4

1 Oberon had put a love spell on Titania. Why did he decide to break the spell?
2 What were Theseus, Hippolyta and Egeus doing in the palace wood?
3 Who did they find there?
4 Why was Egeus angry with Lysander and Hermia?
5 Why wasn't Demetrius angry with Lysander and Hermia?
6 What did Theseus decide the lovers should do?
7 Bottom had some good news for his friends when he came back. What was it?

Act 5

1 Why did the attendant not want Theseus to see the craftsmen's play?
2 Why did Theseus want to see it?
3 Why did Pyramus kill himself in the play?
4 Why did Thisbe kill herself in the play?
5 Why did the fairies come to Theseus's house?

Glossary

1 **playwright** (page 4)
someone who writes plays.

2 **interval** (page 4)
a short break between the parts of something such as a play or concert.

3 **perform** – *to perform* (page 5)
act or sing in front of an audience.

4 **ancient** (page 6)
very old.

5 **characters** (page 6)
a person in a book, play, film, etc.

6 **craftsmen** (page 6)
craftsmen are people who make things with their hands. Quince was a *carpenter* – he made things from wood. Bottom was a *weaver* – he made cloth. Flute was a *bellows-mender* – he fixed things when they got broken. And Snug was a *joiner* – he made the wooden parts of buildings, for example doors and windows.

7 **palace** (page 11)
a large building where kings, queens, or other important leaders live.

8 **fair** (page 11)
beautiful or pretty. In Shakespeare's time, people often used fair before a lady's name when they were talking to them. This was a way of saying something nice to them.

9 **my lord** (page 11)
a polite way of talking to an important person, e.g. a duke.

10 **pretended** – *to pretend* (page 11)
to behave in a particular way because you want someone to believe that something is true when it is not.

11 **nun** (page 13)
a woman who lives in a religious community of women.

12 **praying** – *to pray* (page 13)
talking to God to ask and thank him for things.

13 ***true love*** (page 14)

deep love; when you have very strong feelings about someone.

14 **blame** – *to blame* (page 15)

if you *blame* someone for something, you believe that it is their fault that something bad has happened.

15 **rehearse** – *to rehearse* (page 17)

to practise for a play or concert, or anything which is going to be performed.

16 **parts** (page 17)

the people played by actors in a play, television programme, or film.

17 **comedy** (page 17)

a funny show, television programme – or, in this case, play. In Shakespeare's time, plays were usually either comedies or tragedies. (see below)

18 **cruel** (page 17)

someone who is cruel enjoys causing pain to other people or animals.

19 **mask** (page 17)

something you wear to cover part or all of your face in order to hide who you are.

20 **roar** – *to roar* (page 18)

to make the noise of a lion.

21 **proudly** (page 18)

when someone does or says something proudly, you know that they are very pleased with themselves.

22 **valley** (page 19)

the low land between hills or mountains where a river flows or used to flow.

23 **dewdrops** (page 19)

drops of water which we see on grass and flowers in the morning.

24 **acorn cups** (page 20)

little nuts that grow on oak trees. They are shaped like eggs, with a cover like a little cup on the top. If the fairies could hide in acorn cups, it is easy to imagine how small they were.

25 **cause mischief** – *to cause mischief* (page 20)

to make trouble; to do naughty things, but usually without actually harming anyone.

26 **bless** – *to bless* (page 20)

to say a prayer asking God to help and protect someone or something.

27 **crops** (page 21)

plants that farmers grow in their fields, which we usually eat.

28 **confused** (page 21)

unable to understand something or think clearly about it.

29 **buds** (page 21)

the tightly curled up part of a plant that will open up to form a leaf or flower. Buds usually start to appear in the spring

30 **fault** (page 21)

being responsible for a bad or unpleasant situation.

31 **servant** (page 22)

in old times, people often paid servants to work for them. Servants used to do many different kinds of job, such as cooking food, washing and cleaning.

32 **spell** (page 23)

a magic wish, which makes something strange happen. Spells are usually made by witches or fairies. Sometimes a spell is made just by saying special words. But sometimes, as in this case, a special mixture or object is needed.

33 **iron** (page 23)

a very hard heavy metal.

34 **magnet** (page 23)

a piece of iron that can make other iron objects come to it and stick to it.

35 **master** (page 24)

(in this case) someone who owns and looks after a dog

36 **chased** – *to chase* (page 24)

to follow someone or something quickly in order to catch them.

37 **Athenian** (page 25)

a person who comes from Athens.

38 **bugs** (page 26)

small insects, for example flies and ants.

39 **bats** (page 26)

a small animal that flies at night and looks like a mouse with large wings.

40 **owls** (page 26)

large birds that come out at night. They have big heads and eyes.

41 **sword** (page 29)

a very long sharp metal knife with a short handle. In old times, people used swords for fighting.

42 **making fun of** – *to make fun of* (page 30)

laughing at and making jokes about someone in a way that is unkind.

43 **a gentleman** (page 30)

in old times, a gentleman was a man who was polite and honest and came from a good family.

44 **take part** – *to take part* (page 33)

to join in doing something (in this case, a play) with a group of other people.

45 **donkey** (page 33)

an animal like a small horse, with very long ears. The word *donkey* can also mean someone who is stupid. So when Puck put the donkey's head on Bottom, he was unkindly showing that he thought Bottom was a stupid man.

46 **monster** (page 34)

a large, frightening creature.

47 **make a fool of** – *to make a fool of* (page 35)

when you make a fool of someone, you embarrass them by making them look stupid.

48 **angel** (page 35)

a spirit that in some religions is believed to live in heaven with God. In pictures, angels are shown as beautiful people with wings.

49 **fall in love ... at first sight** – *to fall in love at first sight* (page 35)

when you fall in love with someone at first sight, you start to love them the first time you see them.

50 **foolish** (page 36)

behaving in a way that is stupid and likely to have bad results.

51 **faithful** (page 37)

someone who is faithful stays friends with you, or loves you, even in difficult times. Hermia talks about the sun being faithful to the day, because the sun is there every day.

52 **murdered** (page 37)

killed deliberately. If someone is murdered, you know that the person who killed them wanted them to die.

53 **arrow** (page 38)

a thin straight stick with feathers at one end and a sharp point at the other end. It was used as a weapon in old times. People put *arrows* in a *bow* and shot them at people. Cupid, the ancient god of love, used to have a bow and arrow.

54 **beg** – *to beg* (page 38)

to ask desperately for someone to do something for you or to give you something. When someone begs for something, they want or need it very badly.

55 **mocking** – *to mock* (page 38)

making fun of.

56 **telling the truth** – *to tell the truth* (page 38)

saying what you know is true; not telling lies.

57 **crystal** (page 39)

very expensive, good quality glass. It is usually very clear.

58 **agreement** (page 40)

when you make an agreement, you and another person both promise to do something.

59 **realize** – *to realize* (page 41)

to know and understand something.

60 **stem** (page 41)

the long thin central part of a plant from which the leaves and flowers grow.

61 **prove** – *to prove* (page 42)

show that something is true, for example by doing something (in this case, fighting).

62 **coward** (page 43)

someone who is easily scared, and is not brave.

63 **thief** (page 43)

someone who takes things which belong to another person. Hermia says that Helena is a 'love-thief' because she thinks she has stolen Lysander's love from her.

64 **cheat** – *to cheat* (page 43)

someone who does not behave honestly – and, in this case, someone who takes another person's lover.

65 **puppet** (page 43)

a small toy animal or person. People make puppets move by pulling strings or by putting their hands inside them. Helena calls Hermia a puppet because she is a small woman.

66 **fierce** (page 44)

very angry and frightening to other people.

67 **amazed** – *to amaze* (page 45)

to surprise someone very much.

68 **on purpose**

deliberately; wanting it to happen.

69 **ghosts** (page 46)

strange creatures; some people believe that dead people come to life at night.

70 **stabbing** (page 46)

pushing a knife or sword into something or someone.

71 **playing tricks on** *(someone)* (page 48)

making someone believe something that is not true.

72 **scratch** – *to scratch* (page 50)

(in this case) rubbing part of your body because it feels uncomfortable.

73 **clappers and triangles** (page 50)

the clappers are an instrument made of pieces of wood, which bang together when you shake them. Triangles are metal instruments shaped like triangles, which you bang with another piece of metal. Both the instruments make loud sounds, not beautiful music. Therefore Titania is rather surprised when Bottom says he would like to hear the clappers and triangles.

74 **oats and hay** (page 50)

oats are a kind of grain, and hay is long dried grass. Oats and hay are both used for feeding animals, especially horses.

75 **ivy** (page 50)

a green plant that grows by wrapping itself around trees or other plants.

76 ***shame*** (page 52)
when you do something which makes you embarrassed and sad, you feel shame.

77 ***attendants*** (page 54)
in old times, people who worked for important people such as dukes. Attendants travelled around with their employers, looking after them.

78 **horns** (page 51)
a musical instrument shaped like a tube. One end of the tube is wider than the other end. You blow through the narrow end to play it. Horns are used for *hunting*.

79 ***hunting*** (page 55)
a sport in which people chase after wild animals and kill them. They often use specially-trained dogs.

80 ***melted*** – *to melt* (page 56)
turned into liquid, or disappeared.

81 ***temple*** (page 56)
a place where people of certain religions go to pray. In ancient Greek times, people believed in many different gods, and they went to temples to pray.

82 ***sensible*** (page 60)
reasonable and practical.

83 ***entertainment*** (page 60)
peformances for people to enjoy, for example: plays and music.

84 ***tedious*** (page 60)
long and very boring.

85 ***a tragedy*** (page 60)
a very sad play. Someone usually dies in a tragedy.

86 ***sense*** (page 60)
a way of thinking about something or doing something.

87 ***a speech*** (page 61)
something that you practise saying and then say to an audience or group of important people.

88 ***respect*** (page 61)
liking someone and thinking that they are important and good.

89 ***trumpets*** (page 62)

musical instruments that are like metal tubes with a wide end. You blow into them and press buttons on the top. In Shakespeare's time, trumpets were often played at the beginning of a play.

90 **mantle** (page 62)

a kind of coat used in old times. It did not have any sleeves, and people wore it over their shoulders.

91 **marked** (page 62)

to make a mark on the surface of something so that its appearance is spoiled or damaged.

92 **epilogue** (page 67)

an extra scene at the end of a play.

93 **sweep** – *to sweep* (page 67)

to brush away the dirt with a broom (a long stick with a brush on the end).

94 **applause** (page 68)

when people clap their hands together at the end of a performance to show that they have enjoyed it.

Macmillan Education Limited
4 Crinan Street
London N1 9XW

Companies and representatives throughout the world

Macmillan Readers Pre-Intermediate Level Midsummer Night's Dream, A
ISBN: 978-1-035-15200-1
Macmillan Readers Pre-Intermediate Level Midsummer Night's Dream, A with eBook and Resources
ISBN: 978-1-035-15199-8

This is a retold version by Rachel Bladon of the original work by William Shakespeare.

First published 2007
This edition published 2024

Illustrated by Janos Jantner
Cover photograph by Alamy/Lebrecht Music & Arts

Printed and bound in Brazil
2025
6